A Visit to
IRELAND

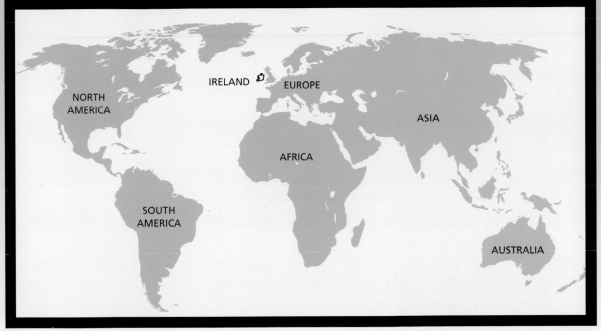

IRELAND
EUROPE
NORTH AMERICA
ASIA
AFRICA
SOUTH AMERICA
AUSTRALIA

Rachael Bell

Heinemann Library
Des Plaines, Illinois

Designed by AMR
Illustrations by Art Construction
Printed and bound in Hong Kong/China by South China Printing Co.

03 02 01 00 99
10 9 8 7 6 5 4 3 2 1

Library of Congress Cataloging-in-Publication Data

Bell, Rachel, 1972-
    Ireland / Rachel Bell.
        p. cm. — (A visit to)
    Includes bibliographical references and index.
    Summary: Provides an overview of Ireland, introducing its land,
landmarks, homes, food, clothes, work, transportation, language,
schools, sports, celebrations, and the arts.
    ISBN 1-57572-847-8 (lib. bdg.)
    1. Ireland—Juvenile literature. [1. Ireland.] I. Title.
II. Series.
DA906.B45 1999
941.5—dc21   98-37707
                                                 CIP
                                                  AC

Acknowledgments
The Publishers would like to thank the following for permission to reproduce photographs:
Brian Kelly p. 23; Collections: Michael Diggin p. 6, George Wright pp. 10, 13, Michael St Maursheil
pp. 14, 20, 25; Hutchison Library: P. Moszynski p. 21; Images Color Library: pp. 7, 26; Image Ireland:
Alain Le Garsmeur pp. 8, 19, Geray Sweeney p. 18; J. Allan Cash pp. 9, 16; Photo Images Ltd:
pp. 11, 24, 27; Rex Features London: Steve Wood p. 15; Robert Harding Picture Library: Duncan
Maxwell p. 17; The Bridgeman Art Library: Board of Trinity College Dublin p. 28; Tony Stone
Worldwide: Oliver Benn p. 5; The Slide File: pp. 12, 22, 29.

Cover photograph reproduced with permission of Tony Stone Images/John Fortunato.

Every effort has been made to contact copyright holders of any material reproduced in this
book. Any omissions will be rectified in subsequent printings if notice is given to the Publisher.

Any words appearing in bold, **like this**, are explained in the Glossary.

Contents

Ireland

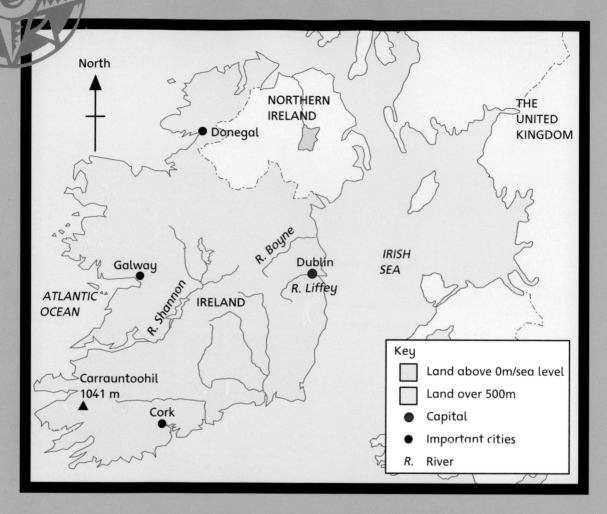

North

NORTHERN IRELAND

THE UNITED KINGDOM

● Donegal

R. Boyne

Dublin ●
R. Liffey

IRISH SEA

Galway ●

ATLANTIC OCEAN

R. Shannon

IRELAND

Carrauntoohil
1041 m ▲

Cork ●

Key

☐ Land above 0m/sea level
☐ Land over 500m
● Capital
● Important cities
R. River

Ireland is on an island in northern **Europe**. Many people live in the country. About one and a half million people live in and around Dublin.

Dublin is the **capital** city. It is on the
Liffey River. The Irish people work, travel,
go to school, and enjoy sports like you.
Irish life is also **unique**.

Land

The center of Ireland is low, flat farmland and **bog**. There are mountains around the coast. These beautiful, rounded mountains are not very high.

The grass and trees are green all year round because it rains a lot. Winds bring clouds from the Atlantic Ocean. These clouds drop rain when they reach Ireland.

Landmarks

There are many **prehistoric sites** in Ireland. The most famous one is at Newgrange. It is more than 4,000 years old. It was built so that sunlight reaches the inside only one day a year.

The Burren is in the west of Ireland. It is a huge, windswept area of rock with underground caves. There is nowhere else like it in all of **Europe**.

Homes

There are still a few **traditional** cottages. They are built from stone and have only one room. They have **thatched** roofs and a plot of land for growing food.

About 150 years ago, landowners forced the
people to leave their land. Many people
died or moved far away. Today many people
are returning to live in the cities and towns.

Food

Irish people usually eat their main
meal at lunchtime. They might have a
Dublin coddle—a stew of sausages,
bacon, onions, and potatoes.

12

The Irish make many different kinds of breads and potato dishes. The **dairies** make very good cheese. There is also lots of fresh seafood.

Clothes

Ireland is famous for its **textiles**. Sheep provide wool which is woven into beautiful clothes. Handmade sweaters are made in Galway. Beautiful **tweed** cloth is made in Donegal.

In recent years, some top **fashion designers** have moved to Dublin. Business is good for the new designers and their shops.

Work

Many farms are small and people grow just enough food for themselves. **Crops** grow better in the east, where it is not so wet. In the west, there are cattle and **dairy** farms.

Many people work in factories, making food or drink. Glass, computers, metals, chemicals, and **textiles** are also made in Ireland.

Transportation

From Ireland, it is easy to travel to and from other parts of **Europe** by both sea and air. Ireland has three **international** airports and its own airline.

Almost all travel within Ireland is by road. There is also the DART, a train that runs along part of the east coast.

languag

English and Irish are the two **official**
languages of Ireland. The Irish
language was brought to Ireland
about 2,000 years ago by people from
Eastern **Europe**.

INIS CIONAITH
WATERFALL 1

km *Cill Mocheanóg*
3 KILMACANOGE

Gleann Cri km
GLENCREE 13

Everyone learns Irish at school. Road
signs and other signs are written in
English and Irish. Some people in western
Ireland speak Irish as their first language.

School

Children go to elementary school between
the ages of six and twelve. The school
day begins at nine in the morning and
ends at about three in the afternoon.

Students go to high school from the ages
of 12 to 15. Their school days are longer,
and they have more homework.

Free Time

Many Irish people enjoy watching or playing sports. Horse races attract huge crowds. Many young people keep their own ponies even in the cities!

On Sunday, some families watch the games of their local sport teams. Hurling is a fast game played with a stick and ball. **Gaelic** football is like soccer, except that the players may hold the ball.

Celebrations

The Irish Derby horse race at Kildare is
held in June. It is an important day for
many Irish people. Horses from all around
the world run in the race.

A special day for **Catholic** children is their First **Communion**. Everyone goes to church in their best clothes.

The Arts

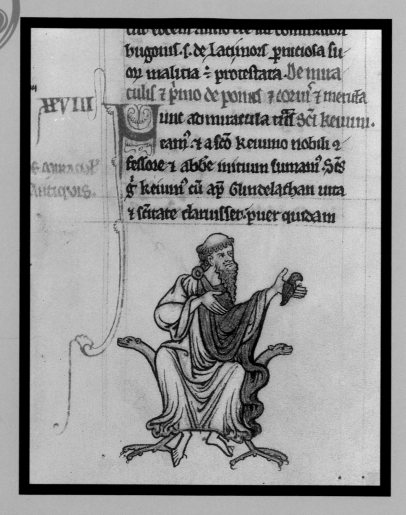

Long ago, each Irish village had its own storyteller. Some of their stories were written down in beautiful books. Many famous writers are from Ireland.

Almost every village has a **traditional** music group. People play the fiddle, the tin whistle, the uileann (yoo-lee-an) pipes, and the bodhrán (bode-ran), a small goatskin drum. They play dance tunes and old **Gaelic** songs.

Fact File

Name The full name of Ireland is the Republic of Ireland.

Capital The **capital** city is Dublin.

Language **Gaelic** Irish and English are the two **official** languages of Ireland.

Population There are about three and a half million people living in Ireland.

Money The Irish have the Irish pound or punt (IR£), which is divided into 100 pence.

Religion Almost all Irish people are **Catholics**. About three out of 100 people are **Protestant**.

Products Ireland produces wheat, barley, potatoes, milk, **livestock**, machinery, and transportation equipment.

Words You Can Learn

aon (ayn)	one
dó (doe)	two
trí (three)	three
tá (thaw)	yes
níl (knee)	no
dia dhuit (dee-a-gwit)	hello
slán agat (slawn-aguth)	goodbye
le do thoil (le-do-hull)	please

Glossary

bog	land that is always wet and spongy
capital	the city where the government is based
Catholic	Christians who have the Pope in Rome as the head of their church
Communion	the Christian ceremony of eating bread and wine
crop	a plant grown and harvested
dairies/dairy	the type of farm that produces milk, cheese, and yogurt
Europe	the continent east of the North Atlantic Ocean and west of Asia
fashion designer	someone who draws ideas for and makes clothes
Gaelic	the language of the people who first lived in Ireland, Wales, and Breton, or describing anything that belonged to them, such as Gaelic music
international	to do with countries all around the world
livestock	animals kept on a farm for their meat or milk
official	decided by the government
prehistoric site	a place where something was located before the time of recorded history
Protestant	Christians who do not have the Pope as the head of their church
textile	cloth or fabric
thatched	made from thick layers of straw or reeds
traditional	the way things have been done or made for a long time
tweed	a thick, woven, wool fabric
unique	different in a special way

Index

More Books to Read

Arnold, Helen. *Ireland*. Chatham, NJ: Raintree Steck-Vaughn. 1995.

Bailey , Donna & Anna Sproule. *Ireland*. Chatham, NJ: Raintree Steck-Vaughn Publishers. 1990.

Benson, Kathleen & Jim Haskins. *Count Your Way Through Ireland*. Minneapolis, MN: Lerner Publishing Group. 1995.